Koheleth speaks!

- Ecclesiastes 3 and 4 -

I0162593

Bob Morris

ISBN: 978-1-78364-513-8

www.obt.org.uk

****

The Open Bible Trust
Fordland Mount, Upper Basildon,
Reading, RG8 8LU, UK.

Koheleth speaks!

- Ecclesiastes 3 and 4 -

Contents

Preface

Preface

In this publication I make several references to the state of affairs in Canada from the Christian, political, moral and ethical points of view. However, Canada is no exception! I am sure the majority of what I have written here is true of many other countries, especially those in the westernised, industrial world. Thus even though the reader may be unfamiliar with the names of certain organisations or individuals, with a little thought I am sure he can find similar ones in his own country.

This book is based upon two sermons I gave at Bendale Bible Chapel, Scarborough, near Toronto in Canada. My prayer is that the reader will find what follows as stimulating and as helpful as the congregation there said they did.

Bob Morris

Ecclesiastes
Chapter 3

Ecclesiastes Chapter 3

1. There is a time for everything, and a season for every activity under heaven:
2. a time to be born and a time to die, a time to plant and a time to uproot,
3. a time to kill and a time to heal, a time to tear down and a time to build,
4. a time to weep and a time to laugh, a time to mourn and a time to dance,
5. a time to scatter stones and a time to gather them, a time to embrace and a time to refrain,
6. a time to search and a time to give up, a time to keep and a time to throw away,
7. a time to tear and a time to mend, a time to be silent and a time to speak,
8. a time to love and a time to hate, a time for war and a time for peace.
9. What does the worker gain from his toil?
10. I have seen the burden God has laid on men.
11. He has made everything beautiful in its time. He has also set eternity in the hearts of men; yet they cannot fathom what God has done from beginning to end.
12. I know that there is nothing better for men than to be happy and do good while they live.
13. That everyone may eat and drink, and find satisfaction in all his toil - this is the gift of God.
14. I know that everything God does will endure for ever; nothing can be added to it and nothing taken from it. God does it so

that men will revere him.

15. Whatever is has already been, and what will be has been before; and God will call the past to account.

16. And I saw something else under the sun: In the place of judgment - wickedness was there, in the place of justice - wickedness was there.

17. I thought in my heart, "God will bring to judgment both the righteous and the wicked, for there will be a time for every activity, a time for every deed."

18. I also thought, "As for men, God tests them so that they may see that they are like the animals.

19. Man's fate is like that of the animals; the same fate awaits them both: As one dies, so dies the other. All have the same breath; man has no advantage over the animal. Everything is meaningless.

20. All go to the same place; all come from dust, and to dust all return.

21. Who knows if the spirit of man rises upward and if the spirit of the animal goes down into the earth?"

22. So I saw that there is nothing better for a man than to enjoy his work, because that is his lot. For who can bring him to see what will happen after him?

Comments
on
Ecclesiastes
Chapter 3

Comments on Ecclesiastes Chapter 3

Ecclesiastes is one of the most modern books in the entire Scriptures. I think if someone had to write an expose, or just a description, of life in the West in the 1990's they would have to write a book very much like Ecclesiastes. The theme which the Teacher "Koheleth" deals with applies to our age, the end of the Twentieth Century in the West, more than to any other society or group of people since this Book was written.

I refer to the writer as *Koheleth* (The Teacher) since it is disputed whether the writer is Solomon or someone else putting words in Solomon's mouth.

Think about it. Who else in Koheleth's day could afford the explorations and the contemplations that he undergoes in Ecclesiastes? Only a very wealthy man, and a man in a place of prominence and power, had the luxury of experimenting with so many different life styles. And it's been true of history ever since. The majority of people are too poor to experiment with hedonism or Epicureanism or stoicism or whatever else you want to describe as the philosophies of life which the writer of Ecclesiastes explored. Most people throughout history, and in fact most people in the world today, struggle every day for the necessities of life - food, clothing and shelter. And it is only the elite, only the wealthy, only the powerful, who have the luxury of sitting back and choosing which life style they should have. And yet in our society, in the

West, in the latter half of the twentieth century, virtually everyone has this luxury.

Virtually everyone in Canada and the whole westernised world today, whether they are unemployed and on welfare or whether they are a fabulously wealthy or powerful person, can choose between a multiplicity of life styles. You can choose to be altruistic or selfish. You can choose to live as if tomorrow would never come or you can live very carefully laying up for yourself treasure. The choices are endless. And in our day we see the results of this experimentation as people in Ecclesiastes day could never have observed it. You can stand in Toronto and observe the meaninglessness of all meaninglessnesses, the vanity of all vanities. They are before us in the experience of people you and I know, and I find Ecclesiastes entirely relevant because we find the same results of the experimentation that Koheleth talks about.

Peter Kreeft, professor of philosophy at Boston College, is one of the people I consulted in thinking about Ecclesiastes. Author of *Three Philosophies of Life*, he says:

> Boredom is the mood of Ecclesiastes. It is a modern mood. Indeed there is no word for boredom in any ancient language. Boredom is a very modern phenomenon. In this mood there is neither a reason to die nor a reason to live and surely this is the deepest pit of all.

In this fear of boredom modern society invents any number of diversions.

Just how modern Ecclesiastes is was impressed upon me recently when I read a novel. It was actually written in 1988 and the novel by Tom Wolfe describes the "go-go" 80's - the days when everybody was making money hand over fist and living as if tomorrow would never come. The hero of this novel, Sherman McCoy, was a wealthy stock broker and, in the beginning of the book, is called *Master of The Universe*. Why? Because on one day Sherman McCoy with one phone call traded some stocks on the stock market and made a fifty thousand dollar commission. He said he could not avoid the feeling that he was *Master of The Universe*. He could merely make a phone call and command fabulous wages and he lived in a 3.2 million dollar condominium in New York City.

In chapter one Sherman McCoy had everything his heart desired and at the time it was money and sex and prestige. 687 pages later in the epilogue to the book, you saw Sherman McCoy being taken in handcuffs to the trial where he was charged with murder, his marriage had collapsed, he was bankrupt, and he was endlessly entangled in court proceedings. And that's how the book ends. There is no end. Vanity of vanities, all is vanity, and it's no mistake that the title of that book, which was subsequently made into a movie, is *The Bonfire of the Vanities*. It's a novel which Ecclesiastes could have written in the 1980s. But other people have written similarly to what Koheleth has written here.

The French existentialist Jean-Paul Sartre, one of the few honest philosophers of the twentieth century, who examined life as it was lived by him and others in Europe, concluded by writing a book called *Nausea*.

Ernest Hemingway that great observer of life, who began as a writer for the *Toronto Star*, ended his own life, in the 70's. He wrote a novel called *The Sun Also Rises*. Now for you and me who understand who created the sun, and who appreciate the providence of God, the sun rising in the morning is a reminder of God's faithfulness to us and His mercies which are new every morning.

But to someone like Ernest Hemingway, visiting the bull fights every day, and trying to escape the boredom of sunny days in Spain, followed by drunken brawls every night, the sun also rising is a curse. It's a condemnation to live a meaningless existence of self-indulgence day after day after day. The sun also rises is in fact a curse and that is a good introduction to the first 15 verses of chapter 3 of Ecclesiastes. If you look at chapter 3, verses 1 and 8 you find that Ecclesiastes is reflecting on the nature of time. Later on he will reflect on the nature of work and then lastly, he will reflect on the nature of death, but his conclusion in every case is "Vanity of vanities, all is vanity". There is only meaninglessness in the cycles of life and of time.

But look at the first fifteen verses where Ecclesiastes is looking at time. Verses 1 to 8 are very popular in 1994. Do you know when I last heard these quoted? I was at a funeral recently, and the service opened with the reading of Ecclesiastes, chapter 3, verses 1 to 8. They are very sedative words aren't they? They are often read in the context of pain and suffering and death. They are a comfort because these words say that no matter what tragedies there are in life they are balanced by joys. No matter what, death comes and life also comes, and time in its endless cycle heals all wounds. For most of us it is a comfort to know that in time our sorrows and our pains will pass. As I began to reflect on this I wondered what it really meant to say, "a time to kill and a time to heal". It was at the time of the murder of an innocent bystander in a Toronto restaurant, and I thought "How can we celebrate that?" Two weeks later we were celebrating D-Day when thousands of people had killed other thousands of people. It was a time to celebrate the heroism and the altruism of those who participated in D-Day, but the force of this cycle of time came to mind. So many of us find comfort in the cycles of time; others find challenge. I've heard this passage quoted in graduations and high school graduation ceremonies. "There's a time for learning, now it's a time for doing". I've heard others find it just a soothing passage, reminding them that whatever troubles are bothering them now, they are just for the moment. They say, time is nature's sedative; in time everything passes and there is a danger that the cycle of time brings a certain pacifity, and pacifity in turn brings what the Preacher calls meaninglessness. It's no mistake that this passage is framed by the last verse of chapter 2: "This too is meaningless, a chasing after the wind", and verse 15, "Whatever is has already been, whatever will be has been before and God will call the past to account". Or, if you look at the footnote, "God calls back the past". There is nothing new under the sun. Life is a cycle; no matter what happens to you, it will pass and something else will come in its place. There's a warning here. Life is cyclical and you will not get meaning for life from time itself. No matter how heroic an action is, it soon will pass and be forgotten. No matter how tragic an event is, it too will pass along with its meaning. Everything happens as intended. Nothing is significant. That's the down side of this beautiful passage and the assumption of the Koheleth throughout Ecclesiastes is that meaninglessness is intolerable.

Human beings cannot live in time and space adequately or fruitfully or happily unless they see meaningfulness and significance in life. In fact, this is the terrible burden that God has placed on man. Look at verse 10. After this marvelous passage on time the Koheleth says, "I have seen the burden God has laid on men". He has made everything beautiful in its time, it is true, but he has also set eternity in the hearts of men. They cannot fathom what God has done from beginning to end. Everything is beautiful in its time but we are more than creatures of time. The burden that God has placed on us is that he has made us creatures of time and space. However, he has also set eternity in the hearts of men, a longing for transcendence, a longing for significance, a longing for the eternal values of God. And the final burden is that no matter how we try, no matter how much we philosophize, or think, or meditate or cogitate or discuss, we cannot fathom what God is doing apart from God's revealing it to us. If we are limited to life under the sun, to mere observation, to our senses, we can never figure it all out.

Think how great a dilemma we have. Our entire environment of life is time and space and yet we are aware of the fact we belong to a 4th spiritual dimension - or a 5th dimension, if we take time as the 4th dimension. Somehow we are creatures who are living in one environment but our spirits, and our souls, and our minds, and our hearts are yearning for something other than time and space. Augustine wrote in his confessions:

> You have made us for yourself and our hearts are restless until they can find peace in you.

And every human being that ever lived is that way. Because we have been created with eternal yearning and yet are limited and living in time and space, we are never satisfied and life does not hold fulfilment for us. Animals are not like that. Have you ever heard a fish complain of being wet? I'm not sure fish even realize they are wet! The environment of the fish is water and they never question it. Marshall McLuhan, who was a philosopher at the University of Toronto when I was there and was very much a guru of the modern media said this, if you can figure it out:

> We don't know who discovered water but we're pretty sure it wasn't a fish.

The last thing we are aware of is our environment and for animals it's absolutely true. They don't question their environment, it just is. Human beings are not like that.

Anything you can observe says we are limited to time and space and yet we have this hunger, this dissatisfaction with time and space, we have this longing because God has set eternity in our hearts and our burden is particularly burdensome in the West at the end of the 20th century because we have tried to secularize all of life. We have tried to remove religion from the public square. We, of all the civilizations on earth, and of all the civilizations that have ever existed on earth, have tried to remove God from public life. Instead of Canada becoming a place of freedom of religion, all our legislation, all our political maneuvering now is to create a country with freedom *from* religion to our own doom. We disallow discussion of values and of Christianity in the public place. We disallow contemplation of the transcendent and the eternal in our public schools. There is no ultimate truth. We tolerate all beliefs as legitimate and we are left with this yawning gap between our experience in what we see and know and that eternity in our hearts which only God can satisfy.

You know, this Book is as modern as yesterday's newspaper. An article by Rick Salutin in Toronto's *Globe and Mail* with the title *The Inexplicable Persistence of Religion* says this:

> I would like to enter a nomination for the most under-rated news story of our time. I nominate as most under-rated story … Religion.

And he describes all the news stories that have happened in the last 12 months which really are based in religion but in which, when the news writers describe them, religion is put in the background. Salutin talks about the political movement of the right in the United States. He talks about all the religiously motivated wars of the last year. He talks about the revival of fundamentalist religion and he says,

You get the impression that news people are more surprised by the prominence of religion today than anyone else. What do they feel, that it was not supposed to happen this way? That we are supposed to live in a secular age? Why does religion persist as a historical force?

Salutin concludes by saying:

> I knew a former Jesuit who theorized that human beings have a need for meaning along with their other basic needs.

Interestingly Salutin didn't come up with that observation himself. He heard a Jesuit Priest once say something like that; every human being has meaning as a basic need. But the heart's cry of every human being that we know in the West is meaninglessness, vanity of vanities, all is vanity. We are so foolish because we have not started with the fear of God which is the beginning of wisdom.

Arnold Toynbee, that famous historian, describes 21 great civilizations in the history of the world, including the western civilization of the 20th century. And he comments,

> Of the 21 great civilizations that have existed on our planet, ours, the modern West, is the first civilization that does not have or teach its citizens any answer to the question of why they exist.

Ecclesiastes is right on. He has exposed our dilemma, the dilemma of our civilization and our society at the end of the 20th century. He begins doing so by his reflection on time, but go on to verses 12 to 14. There he reflects on work; in fact he starts in verse 9. "What does the worker gain from his toil?" He has talked about it in chapters 1 and 2 as well. Look at verses 12 and 13, know there is nothing better for men than to be happy and do good while they live, that everyone may eat and drink and find satisfaction in all his toil. This is the gift of God.

Now here is a very modern problem - verse 9, "What does the worker gain from his toil?" What do you look for from your work? Historically, as I said before, we look for food, clothing and shelter. But the question was never asked. You work because you have to live, that's all there is to it. But in the 20th century we ask for far more. We want to see fulfilment, self fulfilment, job satisfaction. Many of us even find our identity in our work. Have you noticed, particularly with men, how often after they first hear a person's name, they then say "And what do you do?". We do this all the time. I was made more aware of this in the last 2 weeks when even in our Missions we ask the wrong questions of people to see if they are suited for Missions.

A marvellous engineer, Egyptian background, just applied to join *Interserve*, a Christian agency recruiting Christian professionals to work among unreached people. I was really impressed with his resume. He was a senior engineer of Spar Aerospace and the Director of the project that built the space arm for the Space Shuttle, the Canadarm. Now that's impressive! And you start saying to people, "Guess who just applied to Interserve?" But maybe we shouldn't be asking him whether he was the one who put Canada into the Space Shuttle. We should be asking: "Do you beat your wife? Do you love your neighbour?" In our society what you do for a living is so much more important than who you are and what you are like. We have a danger of finding in our work our very identity and our meaningfulness.

The writer of Ecclesiastes is wiser and he says the answer is in verses 12 and 13: here are the things that are good and that you can get from work. You could be happy, you could do good with the money you earn, you may eat and drink and find satisfaction. Now that's quite a bit when you think of it. And that is legitimate, and that is true and that is valid. But what you will not find in your work is ultimate meaning. The rewards are real but there is a certain mechanical existence to work. Look at verse 14:

> I know that everything God does will endure forever, nothing can be added to it and nothing taken from it. God does this so that men will revere Him.

There's a certain limitation to our work, a certain repetitiveness. I've discovered this while my wife is in hospital. She's been there 4 weeks so I do the washing and I do the dusting. You start to see that there's a certain routine here. I dusted only a month ago and it's dusty again already. You know, I did the dishes a week ago and look at them, they're all there again. And you realize that whatever help we get, whatever meaningfulness is extrinsic to the work itself, the work itself is very repetitive and routine and mechanical. Unless we have a purpose in doing the dishes, whether to serve others in our family or to make sure our house is clean or to do it as unto the Lord, work in itself is very mechanical and meaningless and Koheleth understood that. And so for the secular mind it is just as true. He will never find his ultimate purpose in life from his work.

Then thirdly the writer of chapter 3 reflects on death, verses 18-20,

> I also thought, As for men, God tests them so that they may see that they are like the animals. Man's fate is like that of the animals; the same fate awaits them both: As one dies, so dies the other. All have the same breath; man has no advantage over the animal. Everything is meaningless. All go to the same place; all come from dust, and to dust all

return.

And I can hear you protesting in your heart, "But that's not true!" Man is different from the animals. Man is a living spirit. God indwells man, at least potentially. He certainly does in the believers. But think about it - what evidence do you have for that? This was impressed on me two weeks ago when we had a guest preacher at the Church where I usually attend. David Bentley Taylor, 79 years old, lived a good, long, rich life as an overseas missionary. For the last four years he has been nursing his wife, who has been immobilized in hospital and in a nursing home. Earlier this year his wife died. David Bentley Taylor describes that night when he went to bed as usual, (they had given him a bed in the nursing home next door to his wife) but he was awakened at 2 a.m. by the nurse telling him that his wife had died. He says that he went immediately to the room and he looked at his wife very closely, looked at the one to whom three hours earlier he had been reading the scriptures, and comforting and stroking her hair. And he said, she was clearly dead, she was no longer there. There was just a body on the bed, in fact nothing worth more than dumping in the ground. Six times that night he went back to the room and looked at what was left of his wife. And he said:

> Really, looking at her body how could I say that she was any different from the animals? What evidence was there in front of me that she was anything but a corpse at that point in time? Just a body to be disposed of.

And he said it came to him with such force that all he had were the words of Jesus. He had no sensate evidence. Nothing he could see or hear or taste or touch, could argue any differently that his wife was nothing but a carcass. But he remembered the words of Jesus and he quoted John 11:21-26:

"Lord", Martha said to Jesus, "If you had been here my brother would not have died but I know that even now God will give you whatever you ask." Jesus said to her, "Your brother will rise again." Martha answered, "I know he will rise again in the resurrection at the last day." Jesus said to her, "I am the resurrection and the life. He who believes in me will live even though he dies and whoever lives and believes in me, he will never die. Do you believe this?"

Then in verse 40 at the end of the incident Jesus said:

"Did I not tell you that if you believed you would see the glory of God?"

If you limit yourself to what Ecclesiastes has purposely limited himself to, to what the person in our life can see of life and death, we don't have that hope. Life and death themselves do not distinguish man from the animals.

Ecclesiastes' reflections on time and work and death reveal a certain beauty, a certain validity, certain values, to be derived from those three things but they do not provide ultimate meaning for which every human being hungers. How are you and I to respond as God's people in a world like that? You see, that's the world you and I live in with the majority of people reflecting this philosophy, and there is a certain validity to it. There is no need for us to go ranting and raving about the inadequacy of this view of work or time or even life and death. How do we relate?

May I suggest to you first of all we try to understand the mind-set of non-believers. We should try to enter their world and to the extent that their conclusions are valid we should admit them and accept them. I want to talk more about this in the next chapter, where we deal with Ecclesiastes 4. In chapter 4 there is not a single reference to God, there is not one reference to hope, or the future, or eternity. I'm going to suggest that the only way we can relate to what is being said in chapter 4 is to accept what Ecclesiastes says on its own terms. Accept people who say these things at face value and enter their world on their terms if we are really to understand them. That's the first thing we must do as God's people but I suggest on the basis of chapter 3 we should offer more.

We should offer our secularized world, our secular Canada, some glimpse of eternity. We should show people something of the eternal more than time, more than work, more than death. We should become walking audio-visuals of eternity. We should become close encounters of the eternal kind for people who walk in darkness when we walk in the light. We should be to others as creatures not from outer space but from eternal space. Because we are radically different from a non-believer. We are spiritually bi-polar. I don't like to use the word but we are sort of spiritually schizophrenic, half eternal and half mortal. There is in us an eternal spirit which will never die, which is related to the true and living God and real reality. And then there is this mortal flesh which we carry around with us, which one day will be exchanged for something better. But in the meantime we look like everybody else in the world. The only things that make us different are intangible things. Somehow we must open our lives to those who walk in darkness and reveal some of the light to them. We must let them see the elements of eternity which we equate with meaningfulness and significance to those who walk without meaning in their lives. Show our non-Christian friends that knowing God in Christ Jesus transforms not only the next life but the life that is now. Everything is beautiful in its time but there is a beauty and a significance beyond time and space that we must be aware of. Time and work and death are very brief but eternity is not. In John 6:27 Jesus says,

"Do not work for food that spoils but for food that endures for eternal life." We should be living out what Paul talks about in 2 Corinthians 4:18: "So we fix our eyes not on what is seen", (what Ecclesiastes talks about as being under the sun). No! We fix our eyes not on what is under the sun "but on what is unseen. For what is seen is temporary, but what is unseen is eternal."

I know Christians who sort of panic at the idea of leading people to Christ. Just the thought of living in the work place or the neighbourhood or the school or the place of leisure, they panic at the idea of somehow having to share Christ with non-believers and wonder how you do it naturally, how you do it in a way that is effective. I wonder sometimes if our goals are too broad, too high. We think of leading someone from nowhere to a personal relationship to Jesus Christ. What if in this coming week you set yourself the goal of just opening up for one person a glimpse of eternity. Again this was illustrated for me this last week where a colleague of my wife came to the hospital to tell her a story. My wife worked in a pre-school program which is absolutely dead set against any expression of Christianity. Even when the little kids themselves ask to say grace before the lunch time meal, they are forbidden. It's incredible. And this is the politically correct Scarborough Board of Education. But because my wife apparently had had a great influence on her colleagues they meet each week in a grieving session, a time when they get together to work out their own grief at my wife's departure from their place of work. It is a very interesting exercise because there is only one other Christian on the staff. This woman, Dorothy, told my wife Petie just before Petie died that as they were grieving, they were asking Dorothy what they could do to encourage Petie. Someone asked, "What do we have to say to relieve her pain and her suffering?" There was silence so Dorothy took the bull by the horns and loudly and clearly said, "Do you realize Petie gets great strength from her personal relationship to Jesus Christ?" Dead silence. Finally it opened the way to discussion of faith and confidence and what really is meaningful, what really is comforting. Nothing that man can say but everything that God can be for us. And for those people at work for the first time in five years there was a clear testimony to eternal values and the fact that God is on the Throne and Jesus Christ is the Comforter. I assure you that if you can say even the smallest word to point people to Jesus Christ, to life beyond time and space, it will have an impact. Why is that? Because every single human being has been created with this yawning void inside, this hunger for significance, this hunger for meaning which the writer of Ecclesiastes has called eternity, in their hearts and they will respond. You may not observe it but they will see it and think and God will bless it. Jesus said: "I am the Bread of Life, he who comes to Me will never go hungry, he who believes in Me will never be thirsty. I have come that they may have life and that they may have it to the full", and it's that life that we must share with people who live in our world.

Ecclesiastes
Chapter 4

Ecclesiastes
Chapter 4

1. Again I looked and saw all the oppression that was taking place under the sun: I saw the tears of the oppressed - and they have no comforter; power was on the side of their oppressors - and they have no comforter.
2. And I declared that the dead, who had already died, are happier than the living, who are still alive.
3. But better than both is he who has not yet been, who has not seen the evil that is done under the sun.
4. And I saw that all labour and all achievement spring from man's envy of his neighbour. This too is meaningless, a chasing after the wind.
5. The fool folds his hands and ruins himself.
6. Better one handful with tranquillity than two handfuls with toil and chasing after the wind.
7. Again I saw something meaningless under the sun:
8. There was a man all alone; he had neither son nor brother. There was no end to his toil, yet his eyes were not content with his wealth. "For whom am I toiling," he asked, "and why am I depriving myself of enjoyment?" This too is meaningless - a miserable business!
9. Two are better than one, because they have a good return for their work:
10. If one falls down, his friend can help him up. But pity the man who falls and has no-one to help him up!
11. Also, if two lie down together, they will keep warm. But how can one keep warm alone?
12. Though one may be overpowered, two can defend themselves.

A cord of three strands is not quickly broken.

13. Better a poor but wise youth than an old but foolish king who no longer knows how to take warning.

14. The youth may have come from prison to the kingship, or he may have been born in poverty within his kingdom.

15. I saw that all who lived and walked under the sun followed the youth, the king's successor.

16. There was no end to all the people who were before them. But those who came later were not pleased with the successor. This too is meaningless, a chasing after the wind.

Comments on Ecclesiastes Chapter 4

Comments on Ecclesiastes Chapter 4

Chapter 4 of Ecclesiastes is very depressing. It talks of oppression, of unbridled competitiveness. It talks of individualism, it talks about faithlessness and fickle popularity. Unrelieved by hope, unrelieved by any mention of God. There's absolutely no mention of God in this chapter. Now how can one expound that and remain true to the text? My temptation is to immediately move into chapter 5. It starts off so well: "Guard your steps when you go to the House of God, etc., etc." I am tempted to go to that marvellous closing word, that closing chapter 12 beginning at verse 9: "Not only was the teacher wise but he imparted knowledge to the people, etc." But that's not my job. My job is to do chapter 4. I want you with me to set ourselves the goal of looking merely at chapter 4 and perhaps thinking through other things we know of God and his purposes in the world and try to understand the mind and heart of the preacher as he spoke the words of chapter 4.

If we are true to the preacher we can find some momentous conclusions about how to relate to a secular world. The church in Canada and the rest of the westernised world has to change its mind set. For 150 years we have had the luxury of having a country whose laws and customs and social practices and knowledge reflected our own. We are now living at the end of the 20th century as a minority marginalized group of people and we have not become used to that fact. For some reason we are sitting back and looking at the terrible directions Canada is going and wondering why the judges' decisions and the laws of the land, and the parades of Toronto do not reflect our values but values that are very foreign to everything on which this country was based and which makes this country strong. We have not awakened to the fact that our day is past. We are a minority group and I think the preacher today has something to say to us as a minority group in a secular world. Perhaps we have to change our tactics if in fact we are going to be salt and light in that world.

When we look at chapter 4 and the words of Koheleth, we see a certain wisdom and a balance in what he's saying, as painful as it is, and I would suggest to you that Koheleth or the Teacher is not a cynic. The point of view expressed in chapter 4 is not that of a worldly person. It is a believer who is looking at the world that has no hope, a world that does not know God in Christ Jesus and is coming to certain conclusions which he can share with the world. I'm suggesting to you that we have here the realistic believer. He's not living in an ivory tower, he's not living in a monastic cave praising God. He is in fact looking at the world as the secular world will see it, and he is coming to true conclusions which are valid and which we must note. But secondly, having done that, I think we can learn important lessons of how to live in that world as we reflect on it.

Chapter 4 is a celebration of "the better". That word occurs 4 times. Look at verse 3 - "better than both", look at verse 6 - "better one handful", look at verse 9 - "two are better than one", and verse 13 - "better a poor wise youth than an old and foolish king". I think that what we have to do is accept at face value that what Koheleth says is better than what he observed. Now our temptation as God's people is to rush in with God's answer. We want to rush in with the revealed truth that we have in Jesus Christ but I suggest to you that the problem is, the world cannot hear it. The world, because there is a veil over people's eyes and their foolish hearts have been darkened by the evil one, cannot understand or hear God's "best" until we relate to them on the basis of the "better". Chapter 4 is in praise of the better, not the best. If we are going to be realistic in the way we represent Christ in our secular world, I think we are going to have to understand the reality that the world knows only the better. We represent the best and we are going to find that as we look at these four different observations of the preacher, we are constantly going to be wanting to say "Yes, but there's a 'best' way rather than merely a better one." Avoid it - as Archie Bunker used to say in the T.V. show *All in the Family*, - "Stifle!" Stifle the "best" for today, in the interest of the "better" and hopefully the "best" later on. We have to accept the truth that "less is more" when it comes to relating to a secular world.

Let's begin with Koheleth's observations. He starts chapter 4 with, "Again I looked and saw all the oppression that was taking place under the sun" and one of the verses that I did not expound in chapter 3 was verse 16. Think about that one for a minute. Chapter 3 verse 16: "And I saw something else under the sun: In the place of judgment - wickedness was there, in the place of justice - wickedness was there". It's interesting to note what is happening to the judicial system in Canada if you really are concerned about the oppressed of Canada. Have you ever reflected on the discontinuity between righteousness and judgement in Canada, between our law system and morality? We thank God for our country but the Supreme Court of Canada not only preserves and cherishes perverse lifestyles, but protects those perverse lifestyles against any challenge. In fact, in some instances it is trying to force those of us who have other standards to accept people who follow perverse lifestyles as employees. Why is it that the Supreme Court of Canada not only allows, but by their laws encourages, the murder of 90,000 babies per year? That which apparently in Canada is just and legal, is terribly, terribly immoral, and we have gradually arrived at a country where the very legal systems, the political system, and the public values of the secular world, are in direct contradiction to God's law, rather than just being irrelevant. And it is the same in many other countries. We are in a different age and in the very place where judgement and righteousness should be, there wickedness dwells. It is not just in their decisions, it is in their personal lives. In the last six months in the newspapers in Canada we have seen judges accused and convicted of sexual harassment, of bribery, and of perverting justice. So that not only their actions but their individual lives reflect anything but righteousness, and we have to accept the reality of Koheleth's observation on the place of judgement.

But look also at the oppressed:

> I saw the tears of the oppressed - and they have no comforter; power was on the side of their oppressors - and they have no comforter. And I declared that the dead, who had already died, are happier than the living, who are still alive.

Can you challenge that? Recently we have seen new definitions of horror and pain and suffering. The world that previously observed Sudan, and Ethiopia is even more shocked to see Bosnia, Croatia, and Rwanda. Can it get any worse? Yet we go from one escalation of disaster and horror and perniciousness of man's treatment of man, to higher and higher levels of terror and horror. Have you seen the tears of the oppressed? Do you think you can bring comfort to them?

A recent issue of the American *Time* magazine (July 4th 1994 issue), had a remarkable story on battered women and what was remarkable about it was the series of photographs that a woman had taken of people being battered. Somehow she was allowed in these houses and lived with these people to hear their accusations and actually photograph them. One that moved me in particular was the picture of one man leaning over a woman, forcing her head to one side, and the commentary under the picture was that the woman in this picture, tired of the battering she was receiving, sued for divorce and she is now the sole provider for 5 children. And in a small footnote it was noted that the husband has since remarried. Could Koheleth have said it any better?

> I saw the tears of the oppressed and they have no comforter; power was on the side of their oppressors - and they have no comforter.

It is as true today as it was when these words were written and one could easily conclude that those who have died in Rwanda are better off than those who have survived. Can anyone argue against that? And perhaps we are discouraged to think that those who have never been born are better than those who have been. If we look at the evidence before us, if we are realistic, that is the conclusion we must come to. For many people it would have been better that they had never been born and for others, happy are they if they die before they have to subject themselves to the terror that goes on in their countries.

I have to be careful with my next illustration but it's a true one and I don't want to offend people. A newsletter of a sister mission agency came to my desk ten days ago and it was of a ministry which I support and respect. But what they were asking for was for support for the Rwandans. It was virtually right at the height of the slaughter; 500,000 people had been killed by machetes and gun fire and other things. How were they going to help the refugees from

Rwanda? They were asking for donations for fixed-tuned radios to send to the refugees in the refugee camps so that they could listen to Christian programming. Somehow it did not ring true. Somehow I found that even as one who longs to see those people hear the Gospel, I was terribly, deeply, offended. I apologize to the people in that ministry because I understand the legitimacy of their concern. Those radios were requested by people there who were ministering to refugees and there is a certain legitimacy to that ministry. But how do people who are being murdered take comfort from fixed-tuned radios? Have you seen the tears of the oppressed? And before we give them the words of eternal life surely we must take the machetes out of the hands of the killers.

Well, Koheleth moves from the oppressed to the competitive, from the losers to the winners in life, and he makes this observation of the winners:

> I saw that all labour and all achievement (those people who have really achieved anything in this world) spring from man's envy of his neighbour. This too is meaningless, a chasing after the wind. The fool folds his hands and ruins himself. Better one handful with tranquillity than two handfuls with toil and chasing after the wind.

Now unless you are a doctrinaire socialist you have to disagree with Koheleth in his observation. Surely it's not true that all capitalists, and everybody who makes money and everybody who succeeds economically and financially, is an envious, greedy person. We all know altruistic capitalists, don't we? I know people who set out to make money for God's Kingdom. I know people who have succeeded very well in this life, who have a heart for God and for the oppressed so it's not literally true that all labour and all achievements spring from man's envy of his neighbour. But certainly there's a lot of it isn't there? Keeping up with the Jones', wanting to be like the people down the block. There is a lot of greed and a lot of envy amongst people who are making money. So while I can't agree with his extreme statement, my observation matches his that there's a lot of this problem in the world and those who are most competitive and succeed most often have twisted motives and very selfish motives. We can agree with his conclusion. It's not good to be a fool either, and not work. One must have some ambition. But better to be satisfied with one handful than two which is very extreme. And yet (you sort of think in your mind) that's not the way you win gold medals in the Olympics. That's not the way you win a world for Christ. But we shouldn't say that because, "Better one handful with tranquillity than two handfuls with toil and chasing after the wind".

In this third observation, he goes to those who are extreme individualists.

> Again I saw something meaningless under the sun: There was a man all alone; he had neither son nor brother. There was no end to his toil, yet his eyes were not content with his wealth. `For whom am I toiling,' he asked, `and why am I depriving myself of enjoyment?' This too is meaningless - a miserable business!

So Koheleth is observing this and he sees this man with no heir. There's no one to pass on his wealth to. There's no end to his toil. He's a driven man working long hours, probably weekends too, all summer, and hardly taking holidays. He's a driven man, driven to make money and be himself and do it his way. There's absolutely no enjoyment in it. "Why am I depriving myself of enjoyment?" And you notice the one who is earning the money is not making the conclusion. That's the observer who declares this meaningless and a miserable business. It's a miserable business indeed, yet we live in a society in which I would suggest the majority of us believe in individual rights and freedoms, believe and almost sanctify the right of every person to decide for himself and to strive for himself. We admire the self-made man. We glory in individualism in contrast to most cultures of the world which celebrate corporateness and togetherness. And so our society's values reflect this kind of individualism which is concluded as being meaningless and miserable business. The American millionaire Rockefeller was once asked, "How much money does it take to satisfy a man?" Rockefeller's answer was a good one. He said, "Just a little bit more". It's the only thing that will satisfy most of us and no matter how poor we are or how rich. There are very few that do not want a little bit more.

And so Koheleth concludes that two are better than one because they have a good return for their work. Partnership and companionship are better. We can agree with that can't we? I would suggest that these last three verses in this section describe travellers in Palestine. Some have suggested that it might mean marriage. Perhaps, but I think the context is making money and doing business and if one falls into the ditch a friend can help you up. Two of you working together have a better return for your work and if in a cold Palestinian night you find yourself far from home or from an inn, two lying together will keep warm. One may be over-powered by robbers or thieves but two can defend themselves. A cord of three strands is not quickly broken. So there is virtue in co-operation, virtue in getting together and helping one another and that's a value that the world recognizes. So we can agree with verse 9 quite apart from any eternal values but you are tempted to say, "There's so much more than just co-operation with one another". But it's true that two are better than one.

Finally, Koheleth examines the fickleness of popularity in verses 13 to 16:

> Better a poor but wise youth than an old but foolish king who no longer knows how to take warning. The youth may have come from prison to the kingship, (I wonder if he was thinking of Joseph who lived before he wrote this book, perhaps) or he may have been born in poverty within his kingdom. But I saw that all who lived and walked under the sun followed the youth, the king's successor.

No matter how long and rich and famous a life the foolish king had lived, even a poor wise youth was more popular. In due course if the King did not listen to his counsellors and followers, "There was no end to all the people who were before them. But those who came later were not pleased with the successor." And so this is a continual cycle. People come to fame and popularity and the crowds follow them and then later they disappear and their successors are popularly acclaimed and come to power and they too leave and disappear never to be heard of again. I think it was Andy Warhol, the American painter, who said that in the New World, with the media which are instantaneous and global, everyone in the world will have the right to fifteen minutes of fame and then disappear. Joe who? Tanya who? O.J. who? Yassir who? It comes and it goes and its all meaningless, because no matter how famous or how effective or how rich a person is, they too will pass, and others, perhaps less gifted but then more popular will come to power. Still, he's right. "Better a poor but wise youth than an old but foolish king who no longer knows how to take warning".

How can we relate to these observations of a world where the better maybe is the best the world can do. How shall we identify with it? I have come to two conclusions which illustrate how we should respond. I'm not sure they come from this passage; forgive me if they are irrelevant. I suggest to you that Christians must learn in two areas to accept the world's better if we are ever eventually to show them God's best in Jesus Christ. One area is politics and one is in comfort. And I choose these because these are two of the illustrations that come in this chapter.

First of all, think of politics. I began by saying that the church must learn how to live as a minority marginalized group in a secular majority. In Canada today there are two models of what Christians should do politically. I am not telling you to vote a certain way or other. I find it interesting though, that Christians, and particularly Evangelical Christians, have joined the banners of basically two parties. The one is the Reform Party. The other is the Christian Heritage Party. Both a recently formed right-wing political parties in Canada, and Canadian evangelicals see both as representing the Christian agenda.

However, these two parties have very different stances when it comes to moral principles. The Reform Party has accepted the adage that politics is the art of the possible and they are willing to compromise their personal stance, their personal Christian beliefs, in order to identify with a wider group of people who share some of their beliefs but not all of them, and thus have an impact on the Canadian Government and the Canadian people. The Christian Heritage Party, on the other hand, have said that they will stand for uncompromising Christian values. And that's what they have done. Their entire Party program is very distinctly Christian. Unfortunately, because they are a minority group, they have made very little impact. And I suggest to you that if we follow the advice of Koheleth in chapter 4, we will accept something less than the best in order to get something. In politics, as in ministry, sometimes less is more. If we are going to have a wider impact and minister to more people, we may have to compromise our purely Christian standards. I do not mean individually, and I think Preston Manning has set us a marvellous example as has Jake Epp, as has Carmen MacLellan, as has John Reimer, Gerve Fretz and some of the other Christians in Parliament in Canada. They have set a marvellous example of personal integrity, personal lack of compromise on their faith in Jesus Christ. For example, Preston Manning has said publicly many times that he himself is totally opposed to abortion but in Parliament he will go by the vote of his constituency. And you see, Jake Epp's church that supported him in Steinback, Manitoba, totally rejected him because he was part of the government's attempt to get a law passed by Parliament against abortion. They said Jake Epp compromised because that law was going to allow abortions in the case of incest or rape. They asked, "What kind of a Christian is Jake Epp?" Well, Jake Epp's answer to them was that if we don't join with others who are not Christians but who agree that abortion is a terrible smirch on our society, and eliminate as much of it as we can, we won't get anything ... and that's exactly what we got! "All or nothing," they said, and we got nothing! Today, in Canada, we have totally unbridled abortion. Jake has left that church because that congregation has rejected him and questioned his Christianity. At great cost some of these Christian politicians negotiate and accept the limitations of being a minority in a secular world, and they are going to get further ahead than those who insist on purely Christian standards in a world that doesn't accept them.

So politics is one example but I would suggest to you that how we comfort the world, how we minister to the oppressed, is another way that we must accept "better" even though we know "the best". We have to learn how to identify with the oppressed before we prescribe the solution. We have to identify with their suffering, and their killing and their bereavement before we give them radios telling them the gospel. We have to feed them before we preach to them. We have to walk where they walked and accept the silences of God in their life with them and sit with them in that silence before we presume to speak the words of Christ to them. Evangelicals, I think, are always in danger of being accused of having sort of a bumper sticker religion. Christ is the Answer. Simplistic answers to complex problems. I think unless we can see the tears of the oppressed, and sit where they sit, we won't have the right, or the authority, or the opportunity, to share Christ with them. I want to give you three examples.

Forgive me for starting with a personal one but I want to talk just about Christians who are not comforted by other Christians because we fail to accept this principle. Probably the major tragedy of my life happened to me when I was 21 years old. I failed at the University of Toronto and because my very friendly, helpful, fellow-shipping church, Calvary Church in Toronto, identified with me and what I was doing, the most common question on Sunday morning was "How did you do?" Because I'm a little perverse I just said bluntly "I failed". It was amazing to see the reaction of people and how they stammered for words to respond, but their usual recourse was to quote Romans 8:28; "All things work together for good". They had no idea how close they came to getting punched in the face! It got so bad, and I heard Romans 8:28 and 29 so often, I was placing bets with myself that every time I would tell a fellow believer that I failed university he would quote Romans 8:28 to me. Not only did it mean nothing to me, it deeply offended me. Now, looking back I quote Romans 8:28 and 29 because I understand it and I see in fact that it was one of the most formative events in my life, shaping my own relationships to God and to others. God has used that experience in my life to comfort other people. But believers were not ministering to me because I couldn't hear those words when I was in pain.

I saw the movie *Shadowlands* recently, the story of C.S. Lewis' marriage to Joy Davidman and then his bereavement. I commented to a Christian friend of mine that I found it a deeply moving film. I went so far as to say I think non-Christians have done a better job of presenting Christian themes than Christian film makers. I quoted *Chariots of Fire* and *Shadowlands*, and he was deeply offended and he said:

> No! *Shadowlands* is not Christian. It did not reflect the depth of C.S. Lewis' faith. It portrayed C.S. Lewis in rebellion against God and questioning God.

So I thought, I had better test that. I got the book *A Grief Observed* because I wanted to know what C.S. Lewis really did think when he was going through that bereavement. Let me read excerpts from this journal which he wrote in the days following his wife's death.

> Sooner or later I must face the question in plain language; what reason have we except our own desperate wishes to believe that God is good? Doesn't all the evidence suggest exactly just the opposite?

These are the words of a deeply spiritual man who loved God but in his grief wrote these things.

> What chokes every prayer and every hope is the memory of all the prayers Joy and I offered and all the false hopes we had. Not hopes raised merely by our own wishful thinking, hopes encouraged, even forced upon us by false diagnosis, by x-ray photographs, by strange remissions, by one temporary recovery that might have ranked as a miracle. Step, by step, we were led down the garden path. Time after time, when He seemed most gracious, He was really

preparing us for the next torture.

Harsh words.

> What do people mean when they say "I am not afraid of God because I know He is good." Have they never even been to a dentist? Talk to me about the truth of religion and I will listen gladly. Talk to me about the duty of religion and I will listen submissively, but don't come talking to me about the consolations of religion or I shall suspect that you do not understand.

You see, that's the point. It's very difficult to "see the tears of the oppressed" and understand in a way that they will appreciate.

Job's comforters had the same problem. See how they started off well; they came, and as they saw this disfigured man who was their friend, they were in anguish. They sat in sack-cloth and ashes, they struck themselves and they were silent for one week as they sat with Job and commiserated with him. But then they had to start talking. The interesting thing is that everything that Job's comforters said was theologically accurate. I don't think you can read what Job's comforters said and accuse them of unorthodoxy. The only problem with what they said was that it didn't apply to Job in that situation. Neither they nor Job understood what was happening in Job's life, this terrific spiritual warfare, this unseen battle that was taking place around and in Job's life. They had no idea and they started trying to give Biblical answers to a situation that did not match it. Job said to them in verse 3:

> May the day of my birth perish and the night it was said a boy is born, that day may it turn to darkness, may God above not care about it, may no light shine upon it.

He's in despair, and they keep talking to him, telling what the problem is. He must have sinned, how can he be so self-righteous? In Chapter 13 verses 1-5 he says:

> Mine eyes have seen all this, mine ears have heard and understood. What you know I also know, I am not inferior to you, but I desire to speak to the Almighty, to argue my case with God. You, however, smear me with lies, you are worthless physicians, all of you. If only you would be altogether silent. For you that would be wisdom.

Harsh words. But you see Job and all these other people I've illustrated could not hear the best because of their deep pain.

We have to learn somehow to identify with people who have no hope in God, either because they do not know Jesus Christ or because in their deep anguish and suffering and sorrow, they cannot hear it gladly. The word "comfort" comes originally from two words, "cum" which means "with", and "forte" which means "strength". Comfort is just "being strong with someone". It isn't necessarily talking or giving them solutions. Kirkegaard once said:

> If I could prescribe just one remedy for all the ills of the modern world, I would prescribe silence. For even if the Word of God were proclaimed in the modern world, no one would hear it there is so much noise. Therefore create silence.

And that's what Koheleth does in chapter 4 of Ecclesiastes. He gives the silences of God in a secular world and teaches us that if we want eventually to minister to people we must accept their limitations, enter into their sorrows on their terms and accept their analysis of the world and wait for the opportunity to share something better with them. That's how Jesus so often ministered. Did you notice how often He comforted people, and healed them, and never preached the gospel? Did you notice how often Jesus was involved in people's lives and never talked about spiritual things? We are so afraid to do that, aren't we, and yet I believe firmly that is the lesson that God has for us today. He will comfort others with the comfort we have experienced as we enter into their troubles, just as God entered into our troubles and comforted us.

———————————————

More on Ecclesiastes

The Vain and the Sane in Ecclesiastes

Charles Ozanne

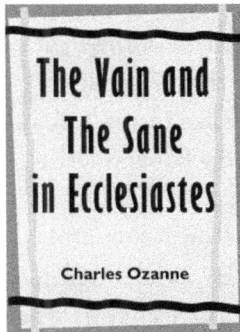

This is an excellent introduction to the whole of Ecclesiastes.

Available as an eBook from Amazon and Apple and as a KDP paperback from Amazon.

For further details please visit

ww.obt.org.uk/charles-ozanne

Also on the Wisdom Literature

The Book of Job: Suffering and the Deep Things of God
by Brain Sherring
The Lesson of the Book of Job—The Oldest Lesson in the World
By E W Bullinger

A Study Guide to Psalm 119
By Michael Penny
Thoughts on Psalm 119
By Ken Clegg
Christ in the Psalms
By W M Henry
Music and Praise in the Life of the Believer
By Brian Sherring

Song of Songs—An Introduction and its Relevance for Today
By Brian Sherring
The Greatest Love Song—A commentary on the Song of Songs
By Brian Sherring
The Song of Songs: An Alternative View
By Sylvia Penny

Details of these books can be seen on **www.obt.org.uk**

They are avaialble as eBooks from Amazon and Apple
and as KDP paperbacks from Amazon.

Free Sample

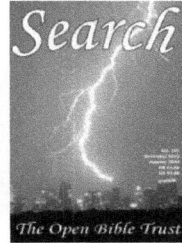

About the Author

Bob Morris was born in Sarnia, Ontario, Canada in 1940. He was educated at Ontario Bible College and The University of Western Ontario. He became a qualified High School teacher and taught for ten years in Canada and overseas. At the time this book was first published (1996) he was a Director of Interserve, a Christian agency recruiting Christian professionals to work among unreached people in closed countries. He was living in both Cyprus and Canada. However, his wife died in 1994, just before the sermons on which this book are based were given. He has two sons.

About this Book

Koheleth speaks!

- Ecclesiastes 3 and 4 -

The author faces the fact that Christians are now in the minority is most westernized countries, and much of the rest of the world. As such we live in a secular society with a desire for pleasure and a fear of boredom. How do Christian survive? And how do they strive for Christian values?

Drawing upon Ecclesiastes - "one of the most modern books in the entire Scripture" - he advocates that Christians would move society closer to Christian values if they met unbelievers where they are, and if Christians were prepared to settle for "better" solutions … rather than going for the "best" or "nothing" scenario.

Publications of The Open Bible Trust must be in accordance with its evangelical, fundamental and dispensational basis. However, beyond this minimum, writers are free to express whatever beliefs they may have as their own understanding, provided that the aim in so doing is to further the object of The Open Bible Trust. A copy of the doctrinal basis is available at

www.obt.org.uk/doctrinal-basis

or from:

THE OPEN BIBLE TRUST
Fordland Mount, Upper Basildon,
Reading, RG8 8LU, UK

www.ingramcontent.com/pod-product-compliance
Lightning Source LLC
Chambersburg PA
CBHW060609030426
42337CB00018B/3014